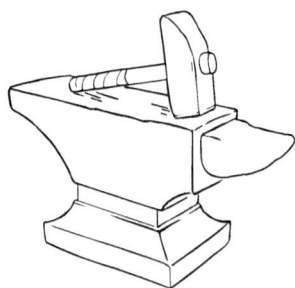

WORLDVIEW GUIDE

GREAT EXPECTATIONS

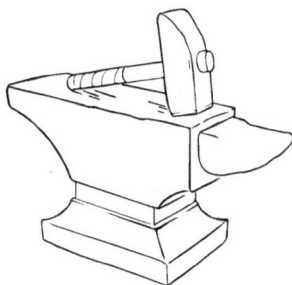

Marcus Schwager

canonpress
Moscow, Idaho

Published by Canon Press
P.O. Box 8729, Moscow, Idaho 83843
800.488.2034 | www.canonpress.com

Marcus Schwager, *Worldview Guide for Great Expectations*
Copyright © 2017 by Marcus Schwager.
For the Canon Classics edition of the novel go to www.canonpress.com/books/
canon-classics.

Cover design by James Engerbretson
Cover illustration by Forrest Dickison
Interior design by Valerie Anne Bost and James Engerbretson

Printed in the United States of America.

A free end-of-book test and answer key are available for download at
www.canonpress.com/ClassicsQuizzes

Schwager, Marcus, author.
Great expectations worldview guide / Marcus Schwager.
Moscow, Idaho : Canon Press, [2017].
LCCN 2019011330 | ISBN 9781944503956 (paperback : alk. paper)
LCSH: Dickens, Charles, 1812-1870. Great expectations.
LCC PR4560 .S39 2017 | DDC 823/.8--dc23
LC record available at https://lccn.loc.gov/2019011330

17 18 19 20 21 22   9 8 7 6 5 4 3 2 1

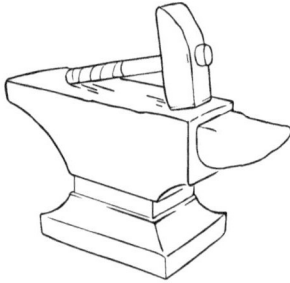

CONTENTS

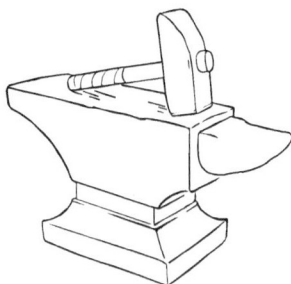

INTRODUCTION

It's the early 1800s; you're a young boy growing up in the poor slop of the rural moors in England. You take a quick walk from your cottage to visit family graves and are caught up by a snarling, escaped convict threatening to have your beating heart dug out if you don't obey his every word. Now imagine, over the next few years, that you silently, privately hand your soul to the girl of your dreams . . . who delights in slowly, carefully breaking and digesting your heart for her own perverse pleasure. Then, as you approach adulthood, imagine that convict anonymously showering you with all the wealth he never had. And imagine that young woman finally, kindly, lovingly, restoring that pulpy, innocent heart to you. This is Philip Pirrip's life of *Great Expectations*. Join us as we wander through a rich masterpiece of England's wondrous storyteller, Charles Dickens.

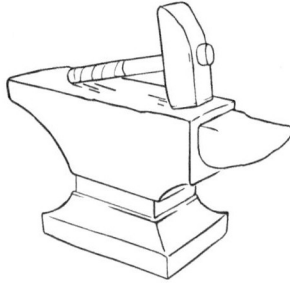

THE WORLD AROUND

Great Expectations is a perfect title for the contextual era of its composition, Victorian England. Many English cities were transformed from quiet, coastal dwellings of local trade, farming, and apprenticeship to economic powerhouses through global trade expansion, canal and railway distribution, and factory production hungry for low-wage, unskilled labor. Thousands of middle-class families ventured to hitherto unreachable social heights through business. But thousands more poor families flocked to filthy city ghettos searching for work as the old fabric of rural life unraveled.

The results were, simultaneously, an unprecedented increase in general luxury (electric lighting, park picnics, museum strolling, telegraph communication, and train service all spring up in this era) and general squalor (oppressive child labor, extensive pollution, overflowing street-side sewage, and mass spread of disease among the poor). From the outside, England seemed to have come into its own; perhaps the greatest power on earth, it drew on resources from its territories around the globe. But on closer examination, one wondered, had a world of great expectations come at the loss of a nation's soul?

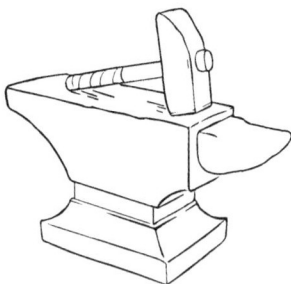

ABOUT THE AUTHOR

Charles John Huffam Dickens (1812–1870) was born into humble circumstances in Landport, England. He had little education as his family often moved due to financial strain caused by his father's modest salary and financial incompetence, which finally landed the family in debtor's prison. Charles was thrown into 10-hour workday factory labor at age twelve to help the family survive. The shame and trouble of this period in Dickens's life left an indelible mark on the mind of our future author.

At age twenty, Dickens tried his hand at acting and writing short pieces; he found more success in the latter, becoming a political journalist sketching colorful scenes from the House of Commons. Those *Sketches by Boz* (written 1833–36; "Boz" being an early pen name) granted him opportunity to move into wider fields of creative writing. Since he wrote for weekly publication by installment, he could gauge his writing by popular response and adjust accordingly. For instance, his first novel, *The Pickwick Papers* (1836), got off to a slow start. But when he introduced a gloriously fun Cockney character, Sam Weller[1] in chapter 10, sales took off. Dickens took note, drawing rich, colorful, humorous characters into his work henceforth, and his career skyrocketed. Contrasting his father, Charles Dickens was exceptionally shrewd, financially. He would serialize his writing weekly, then publish it as a complete work, and finally give dramatic performances of various scenes on tour, often earning profits at least three times on the material.

The year of Pickwick's publication, he married Catherine Hogarth. Their twenty-two years of marriage brought ten children. Over the course of his career, Dickens produced 20 novels, 5 novellas, and hundreds of short stories, articles, lectures, and performances. He deserves particular credit for his concern for children, spending much energy to secure better lives and working conditions for England's impoverished young.

Unfortunately, Charles and Catherine Dickens separated in 1858, Charles having fallen for a young actress he had hired. His prolific output, too, came at a cost; he knew virtually no rest for decades, and likely worked himself to death. As an adult, he is said to have always appeared ten

---

1. For example, consider this famous Wellerism from *The Pickwick Papers*: "Vich I call addin' insult to injury, as the parrot said ven they not only took him from his native land, but made him talk the English langwidge arterwards."

years older than his actual age. In his last years of traveling and lecturing (late 1860s), he suffered fits of paralysis, which escalated into strokes. He suffered his final stroke on June 8, 1870, after a hard day's work on *Edwin Drood*. He never regained consciousness, dying the following day, age fifty-eight. Although he gave explicit direction that he should have a quiet and modest burial, he was laid to rest in the illustrious Poets' Corner of Westminster Abbey.

Charles Dickens is England's greatest Victorian novelist and deservedly within the pantheon of her finest writers. His pathos, personality, wit, poetry, and plotline make him a direct descendant of England's literary greatness, particularly reminiscent of William Shakespeare, Sir Walter Scott, and John Keats. In fact, the very tones and textures the world knows of Britain—from the grand and sentimental "merry old England" to a colorful array of exaggerated characters—owe their origins to Dickens. Dickens's imaginative genius brought the world Ebenezer Scrooge, Mr. Jarvis Lorry, the Artful Dodger, Miss Havisham, and so many other fine characters, richly supplying and embellishing Britain's cultural and character stockade that had been first provisioned by Geoffrey Chaucer's motley pilgrims in *The Canterbury Tales*.

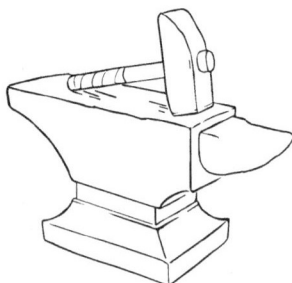

WHAT OTHER
NOTABLES SAID

"Whatever the word *great* means, Dickens was what it means." ~ G. K. Chesterton in his biography *Charles Dickens* (published 1906)

"In the case of Dickens [picturing him based on what he wrote], I see a face that is not quite the face of Dickens's photographs, though it resembles it. It is the face of a man of about forty, with a small beard and a high colour. He is laughing, with a touch of anger in his laughter, but no triumph, no malignity. It is the face of a man who is always fighting against something, but who fights in the open and is not frightened, the face of a man who is generously angry." ~ George Orwell in his biography *Charles Dickens* (published 1940)

"[Dickens] is, by the pure force of genius, one of the greatest writers of the world... There is no 'greatest

book' of Dickens; all his books form one great life-work: a Bible in fact…all are magnificent."
~ George Bernard Shaw[2]

"Dickens more than any of his contemporaries was the expression of the conscience … of his age …. Any account of Dickens is inadequate. He is the greatest comic novelist in English; he is also the truly poetic novelist." ~ Walter Allen in *The English Novel*

---

2. Edgar Johnson, "The Dying and the Undying Voice." From *Charles Dickens: His Tragedy and Triumph* (New York, 1952, 2 vols.), later included in *Charles Dickens: New Perspectives*, edited by Wendell Stacy Johnson (Edgewood Cliffs, N.J.: Prentice-Hall, 1982).

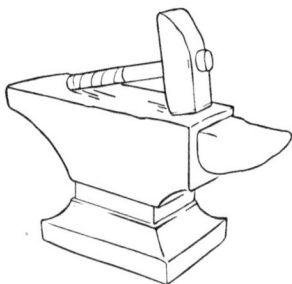

PLOT SUMMARY, SETTING, AND CHARACTERS

- *Setting: England, early 1800s. The tale begins in the rural moors of Kent, some miles from the River Thames at the forge and humble cottage of the Gargerys, takes a few turns about Miss Havisham's declining manor house, and proceeds to the urban jumble of London. The tale then ends back in the country at the Gargerys' and the now utterly ruined Satis House (Miss Havisham's).*

- *Philip Pirrip:* Protagonist and narrator of the novel. Our tale opens when he is about seven years old. He never knew his father and mother (they both died before Pip could know them) and is "raised by hand" by his sister, Mrs. Gargery, a hard and insensitive woman. The novel follows his life at various stages from this time on and finally ends with Pip in his mid-30's.

- *Mrs. Joe (Georgiana Maria):* Pip's sister and guardian upon the death of their parents. She treats Pip and her husband Joe severely. Later in the novel, she is attacked by Orlick and suffers severe mental and physical effects rendering her disabled until her death.

- *Joe Gargery:* A kind, virtuous, gentle, and uneducated blacksmith who raises Pip with his wife, Georgiana (Mrs. Joe). After Georgiana dies, he will marry Biddy.

- *Biddy:* A sweet, intelligent, poor, benevolent companion of Pip who works at a nearby evening school and teaches Pip all she knows. Pip doesn't recognize her value or the love and esteem that she holds for him, as he's taken by the alluring Estella. Later, Biddy marries Joe Gargery.

- *Dolge Orlick:* The rude, vengeful journeyman under Joe at the forge. He attacks Mrs. Joe so violently that she never recovers. He also lures Pip into a trap with murderous intentions, but Pip is rescued by three friends. Orlick's violent crimes go unpunished, though he will later go to prison for another offense.

- *Abel Magwitch (alias Provis):* A surly escaped convict who threatens Pip's life in the opening of the novel. Later, Magwitch becomes Pip's mysterious (and anonymous) benefactor. He was once in league with the dashing conman Compeyson, but being betrayed, hates the man fiercely.

- *Miss Havisham:* A jilted (by Compeyson) spinster who resides in a great dark manor house and brewery, allowing it to fall into disrepair. Her clocks, food, dress, and home decoration all remain the same as the moment she was left at the wedding altar. She raises Estella to take revenge on men, to mercilessly break their hearts as her heart was broken. Miss Havisham's festering hate and anger has transformed her into a corpse bride.
- *Estella:* The beautiful adopted daughter of Miss Havisham. Estella is bred to torment men and break their hearts. Later, we learn that she is actually the daughter of Magwitch and Molly (Jagger's servant).

The easiest way to make sense of the many characters and subplots is to begin with the heart of the novel. At its core, we have a protagonist, Pip, developing in the distant context of two father figures, Joe Gargery the blacksmith and Abel Magwitch the convict. The plot arc follows the three stages of Pip's development: (1) childhood, (2) elevation to great (social) expectations, (3) revelation of the truth. Pip's character motivation centers on his desire for Estella's hand in marriage and his social ambitions to help secure that coveted relationship. Thus, the father figures provide the structural background, and the love interest the immediate emotional foreground of the work.

The story opens on Christmas Eve in the early 1800s. Our narrator and protagonist, Pip, is seven years old, and visiting his family grave near the humble cottage and forge where he has grown up in the moors some miles off the River Thames. A convict lurches from behind a tombstone and catches poor Pip, demanding "wittles" (food) and a file (to open the shackles), else dire consequences will follow. Pip obeys the convict, sneaking the necessities from his home and forge for the convict, Abel Magwitch. The next day, Magwitch is found fighting another escaped convict, Compeyson. Magwitch is willing to lose his own freedom to secure the imprisonment of this enemy.

Pip's parents are long dead and his guardians are opposing forces: Georgiana (Mrs. Joe) is rough and rude to her younger brother Pip, claiming to bring him up "by hand," but generally abusing her authority and injuring his sensitive nature. Joe Gargery (her husband, the blacksmith) on the other hand, is a mighty, uneducated, wise, gentle ox of a man. He treats Pip tenderly and as an equal, yet will not correct the excesses of his domineering wife, lest he hurt her. So life goes on for Pip. He shares a rich connection to Joe, but a complication occurs when Pip is invited to meet with a well-to-do young lady (Estella) at Satis House. Miss Havisham keeps a curious house, decaying midst the old remnants of a finely set but untouched, rotting wedding day celebration. Little does Pip know that Miss Havisham was jilted long ago and has raised Estella to break men's hearts. Pip takes the bait, admiring Estella, yet burning with a sense of inferiority.

Still, Pip remains at Joe's side, and enjoys advice and help from Biddy, a country friend. Pip becomes apprenticed to Joe as a forger (typically, age fourteen), but as his teen years progress, a lawyer visits to inform Pip that he has an inheritance from an anonymous source: great expectations have fallen to the humble blacksmith's apprentice. For Pip, this means that he can become a true gentleman and hope to win a future with the young lady of his dreams, Estella. Pip turns his back on his humble past and embraces the "gentleman's" life in London, spending his inheritance foolishly and finally coming into great debt. In the meantime, Pip's sister, Mrs. Joe, is attacked by Joe's journeyman Orlick, leaving her seriously disabled. She never recovers and finally passes away.

On his twenty-third birthday, Pip is visited by a strange character who turns out to be none other than Abel Magwitch, the convict who had threatened Pip at the outset of the novel. Astonishingly, this convict has been Pip's benefactor, Magwitch aiming to invent a gentleman rather as Miss Havisham created a cruel mantrap in Estella (Havisham begs forgiveness for this from Pip just before she dies in this section of the novel; Pip freely forgives her). Immediately repulsed by the thought that his great expectations came from such sordid sources, Pip still agrees to help Magwitch escape London. The scheme of escape fails, and Magwitch is cast into prison where he soon dies, a humbled Pip attending him.

Pip falls ill himself, his old paternal figure Joe Gargery tending him and paying off his debts. A repentant Pip decides to return to his rural home to consider picking up blacksmithing with Joe and marrying the childhood girl, Biddy, who had once admired him, but whom he had neglected. Sadly, for Pip, Biddy is already marrying Joe, and Pip is rather past the age of apprenticeship (typically ending at age twenty-one). Pip travels to the east to work with a friend Herbert Pocket.

Eleven years later, Pip (now thirty-four) returns to visit Joe and Biddy and take a look at his old haunts. He then takes a stroll by Satis House, or more accurately the property, the once-decaying structures having been cleared for new development. In the evening mists, Pip makes out a figure. It's Estella taking a last look over the site herself. Year ago, Estella had married Drummle, a man even more cruel than she. The experience brought her wisdom, albeit through sad, painful means. Drummle dies young, and Estella is left a widow. She, too, sought and received forgiveness from Pip. Pip and Estella now openly share their care for one another, and Pip concludes: "I took her hand in mine, and we went out of the ruined place; and, as the morning mists had risen long ago when I first left the forge, so the evening mists were rising now, and in all the broad expanse of tranquil light they showed to me, I saw the shadow of no parting from her."

That final line ought to give you goosebumps no matter who you are.

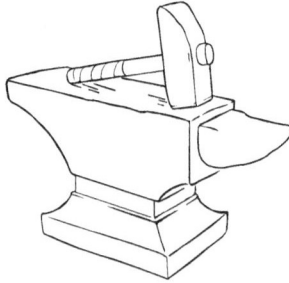

WORLDVIEW ANALYSIS

Charles Dickens was baptized and raised in the Church of
England; aside from a Unitarian season in the 1840s, he
attended Anglican services throughout his life and prayed
each morning and evening. He deeply revered Christ Je-
sus and the teachings of the New Testament, but, sharing
a common Victorian intellectual prejudice, showed little
tolerance for church dogma, Old Testament morality, or
sectarian zeal (whether Evangelical or Roman Catholic).
For many Victorian thinkers, the Old Testament Jehovah
represented a wrathful legal justice while Christ's New
Covenant revealed the way of mercy and peace. While
this reading is quite short-sighted and even anti-Trinitari-
an, it provided a means to cordon off aspects of traditional
faith (whether hell, damnation, superstition, Judaism, cap-
ital punishment, the Genesis account of creation, or the
sacrificial system) deemed obnoxious, evil, or outmoded

by Victorians who could not see a way to reconcile various biblical, historical, and scientific positions.

Dickens's faith clearly directed his labors, perhaps to a much deeper level than many readers imagine. Consider this excerpt from a letter he wrote to Reverend Macrae:

> With a deep sense of my great responsibility always upon me when I exercise my art, one of my most constant and most earnest endeavours has been to exhibit in all my good people some faint reflections of our great Master, and unostentatiously to lead the reader up to those teachings as the great source of all moral goodness. All my strongest illustrations are drawn from the New Testament; all my social abuses are shown as departures from its spirit; all my good people are humble, charitable, faithful, and forgiving. Over and over again, I claim them in express words as disciples of the Founder of our religion; but I must admit that to a man (or a woman) they all arise and wash their faces, and do not appear unto men to fast.[3]

Thus, Dickens hoped to direct his readers' hearts toward Christ without obviously seeming to do so. He did write one overtly religious book, *The Life of Our Lord*, but did not intend it for his reading public.[4]

---

3. From David Cody's article "Dickens and Religion" (see victorianweb. org).

4. *The Life of Our Lord* was an account of the gospels for him to read to his children. He finished it in 1849, but requested that it not be made available to the public for eighty-five years.

This background illuminates the fact that so many of Dickens's characters and scenarios illustrate themes of forgiveness, revenge, atonement, sacrifice, pride, love, and humility, all happening within the heart and between characters rather than mediated through any particular church or traditional religious experience. Something deeply Romantic ever stirred in the great heart of our author, both for good and for ill.

In *Great Expectations*, we may work our way out from the title. Solomon knew that "the blessing of the Lord makes one rich, and he adds no sorrow with it" (Prov. 10:22), that "an inheritance gained hastily at the beginning will not be blessed at the end" (Prov. 20:21). Pip discovered the sorrow that accompanies an encouraged and flattered zeal unchecked by patience, consideration, or maturity. He learned that resources hard-earned by a progenitor can be easily squandered by an inheritor. In this way, the prodigal son overlooks the love and kindness and provision he has at home to reach apparently richer vistas of excitement far off—only to learn that true impoverishment is not found in the humble blacksmith's cottage, but in the company of the jilted who go on jilting one another. Pip's homecoming strikes a more bittersweet note, as he has lost people and possibilities (such as Biddy) that cannot be regained. However the passion he entertained for Estella does finally mellow into wisdom, and God deems fit to grant him a great inheritance in love that will cause no more sorrow, which he will not squander. So Pip does finally come into real and *good* expectations, now that he is humble enough to no longer burn for *great* expectations.

Dickens's chief means of finding humility are seeking, receiving, and extending grace. This novel's focus on forgiveness is pervasive, even relentless.[5] Joe Gargery is perhaps the most gracious and forgiving character in the novel, the true gentle man. Whether attacked, belittled, ignored, snubbed, or disappointed, he remains kind and generous. The only moments in the novel where anything like rudeness erupts are when his love and dedication to Pip are construed or implied to be self-serving or for financial gain. He plays the role of the prodigal's welcoming, understanding father who receives Pip even after Pip repeatedly ignored and abandoned his one-time trade master. Estella and Miss Havisham are both desperate to receive absolution from Pip for having tortured his young heart. They are both forgiven, of course (see Quotables section). But it is too late for Miss Havisham to know more in life than that, for while she softens toward Pip and sees her sin toward Estella, the burning hatred she bore so long for her jilter Compeyson finally consumes her in a blaze of fire. Estella, though, has hope; indeed, her warped mind was more acted upon than acting, and

---

5. Forgiveness might have been on his mind a good deal as this novel was published just three years after Dickens left a marriage of 22 years for an affair with an 18-year-old actress (he was then 45).

she has realized what devastation brutality brings to love in her own early marriage.[6]

Those who cannot forgive (Miss Havisham with Compeyson, or Abel Magwitch with the same man, or Orlick with anyone) are doomed on earth, yet ultimate redemption may still be theirs if they can admit their wrong and seek grace and restitution. So Abel Magwitch kills Compeyson and dies in prison, sick and awaiting execution, but his heart has known grace in his dealings with Pip; his final moments are quiet, peaceful, and "placid," knowing good news from Pip's lips concerning his long-lost daughter. The chapter concludes with Pip's prayer: "I thought of the two men who went up into the Temple to pray, and I knew there were no better words that I could say beside his bed, than 'O Lord, be merciful to him, a sinner!'"

The mercy and grace characters seek, find, and extend in the novel create the deeper relationships and riches that transcend bonds of class, creed, or blood. In the end, Dickens highlights the truly great expectations one only finds in grace and forgiveness.

---

6. Both Mrs. Joe and Estella appear to grow humbler under the hand of heavy abuse, which is a sad coincidence from Dickens (and rather melodramatic to boot).

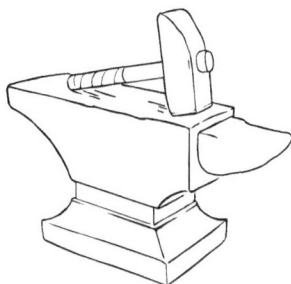

QUOTABLES

1. "Her contempt for me was so strong, that it became infectious, and I caught it."

2. "Ask no questions, and you'll be told no lies."

3. "I loved her against reason, against promise, against peace, against hope, against happiness, against all discouragement that could be."

4. "Heaven knows we need never be ashamed of our tears, for they are rain upon the blinding dust of earth, overlying our hard hearts."

5. "Love her, love her, love her! If she favours you, love her. If she wounds you, love her. If she tears your heart to pieces—and as it gets older and stronger, it will tear deeper—love her, love her, love her!"

6. "My name is on the first leaf. If you can ever write un-
    der my name, 'I forgive her,' though ever so long after
    my broken heart is dust, pray do it!"

    "O Miss Havisham," said I, "I can do it now. There
    have been sore mistakes; and my life has been a blind
    and thankless one; and I want forgiveness and direction
    far too much, to be bitter with you."

7. "There was a gay fiction among us that we were con-
    stantly enjoying ourselves, and a skeleton truth that we
    never did. To the best of my belief, our case was in the
    last respect a rather common one."

8. "No man who was not a true gentleman at heart,
    ever was, since the world began, a true gentleman in
    manner."

9. "My Lord, I have received my sentence of death from
    the Almighty, but I bow to yours."

10. "O dear old Pip, old chap," said Joe. "God knows as I
    forgive you, if I have anythink to forgive!"

11. "But you said to me," returned Estella, very earnestly,
    "'God bless you, God forgive you!'"

12. "Suffering has been stronger than all other teaching,
    and has taught me to understand what your heart used
    to be. I have been bent and broken, but—I hope—into
    a better shape."

13. "I took her hand in mine, and we went out of the ruined place; and, as the morning mists had risen long ago when I first left the forge, so the evening mists were rising now, and in all the broad expanse of tranquil light they showed to me, I saw the shadow of no parting from her."

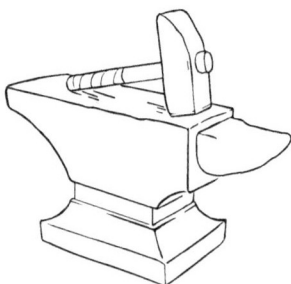

21 SIGNIFICANT
QUESTIONS AND ANSWERS

1. Why begin this tale on Christmas Eve?

    Dickens masterfully moves his readers' emotions
    by creating contrast in holiday seasons (consider
    A Christmas Carol). Here, we have the expected
    convivial warmth of Christmas Eve contrasting
    the cold horror of the Pip's actual circumstances.
    Rather than celebrating the birth of a poor baby
    boy, we nearly witness the death of a little Pip.
    Comparatively, both Jesus and Pip come from hum-
    ble places, social outliers of uncertain parentage.

2. Compare and contrast Magwitch and Compeyson.

    Superficially, both men are convicted criminals.
    They worked together in a counterfeiting scheme
    for which they were incarcerated. The men hold an
    abiding hate for one another and will not forgive or

relent. Beyond that, they are very different characters. Compeyson is refined, educated, clever, and cunning. Magwitch is coarse and direct, having grown up poor and uneducated. Even though the counterfeiting scheme was Compeyson's plan, he serves less time (seven years) than Magwitch (fourteen years) due to leniency shown for his higher social standing.

3. When does Pip become ashamed of his humble background? Why?

When Pip visits Miss Havisham and meets Estella, he becomes embarrassed by his humble circumstances largely because he wants to engage Estella on a more equal footing, hoping to win her heart someday.

4. Which character beside Pip seems most vivid and interesting to you? Explain.

Answers will vary. Dickens is a master of the caricatured character, peopling the literary landscape with a wide array of memorable characters.

5. Who is the finest gentleman in the novel? Explain.

This is a challenging question, as there is no clear gentleman in every sense of the word. Those who appear to be or put themselves forward as being elite gentlemen (Compeyson, Mr. Pumblechook, Bentley Drummle) are nothing of the sort, morally, while other characters who cannot aspire socially or educationally to a gentleman's status (such as Joe Gargery) show the best marks of truly gentle men. Perhaps Pip's friend, Herbert Pocket, provides the nearest balance both socially and morally; otherwise, Joe is probably the best choice. Some readers may even choose the convict Magwitch due to his final reformation and kindness to Pip. Other choices are possible.

6. Who or what is the antagonist in the novel?

This is another complicated concern. The opening of the novel points to Magwitch, then Orlick, as the likely chief antagonists. One might make a case that even when Magwitch financially supports Pip, he serves him antagonistically, since Pip descends further and further into moral failure through this support. Still, that's a stretch, since for most of the novel Miss Havisham and Estella (ruled by Miss Havisham's stratagem) serve as the obvious antagonists, trapping Pip into impossible expectations in order to break his heart. A third view, and perhaps the most satisfactory in that it holds for most of the novel, is that Pip's gullibility and weak character serve as the antagonist to his success. From his early trail with Magwitch to his hopes for Estella to reckless bachelor living, Pip evinces serious credulity as he misreads and improperly values nearly every relationship and opportunity that comes before him. *Great Expectations* is a true coming-of-age (also called "*bildungsroman*") novel where the reader witnesses naïve character grow into a gracious and seasoned manhood.

7. Who is the chief villain in the novel? Is this character the same as the antagonist? Why or why not?

    > The most villainous characters are Orlick (beats Mrs. Joe dreadfully tries to murder Pip), Compeyson (destroys Miss Havisham; continues his life of crime) and Bentley Drummle (abuses Estella), but, while they are antagonists, they are not the chief antagonists of the novel.

8. Which characters show forgiveness in the novel? Which characters do not? What do we see when we compare these characters (beside the fact that they do or do not forgive)?

    > Joe (to Pip), Biddy (to Pip) and Pip (to Magwitch, Miss Havisham, and Estella) all extend a great deal of forgiveness. Miss Havisham seeks forgiveness but can never forgive those who jilt her. Magwitch deals kindly with Pip but cannot quench his undying hate for Compeyson. Compeyson will not seek amends or forgive Magwitch. Orlick will not forgive Pip for causing him to lose work at Satis House. Each of the latter characters die violently or are imprisoned indefinitely.

9. Do you think that Dickens is teaching that it is wrong to try to better oneself socially? Why or why not?

    > In the end, Herbert Pocket and Pip both find means of honestly sustaining a higher social place.

It seems unlikely that Dickens is against social improvement, generally, as his own life testifies to such improvement and his works seek to remedy injustice but not discourage better lives. Pip's error was not so much in dreaming beyond the forge but in improperly valuing it and Joe. Or, from another view, money is not the means to higher living and moral character; it's often the reverse. Still, aspiring for greater education, nobility, and influence in the world can be commendable and also produce wealth in the process. But when money becomes a substitute for labor, character, and honor, little good will come of it.

10. Dickens is a master of metaphor. Often, a character is likened unto an animal (Magwitch to a nervous dog eating, Pumblechook's mouth to a fish). Jaggers, the astute lawyer, calls Drummle a "spider." How is Drummle a spider in the novel?

> While Estella was raised to trap men and hurt them, she meets an even worse person in Drummle. Like a spider, he traps her, spins her into his home, and draws the life out of her by his abuse.

11. How is Pip like the prodigal son (Luke 15:11-32)?

> Pip leaves home unwisely to spend his money lavishly in company that (mostly) encourages lazy, foolish, and corrupt character. Having spent beyond his means, he finds himself in great debt, destitute and sick. He is brought back to life through the

generosity, love, and forgiveness of his father figure,
Joe. Pip realizes that he has acted foolishly and only
wants to come home; however, home has changed
for Joe and Biddy, and though he is loved, Pip
must move on (this final clause in contrast to the
prodigal's tale).

12. How does this tale echo elements of the fairy tale
"Cinderella"?

Pip is the poor working child who is harassed by a
stepmother of sorts (in his case, a much older sister). Initially unable to enter the higher social world
(to approach the girl his hopes and affections are
set on), Pip is visited with unlooked-for resources,
magically. This "magic" brings complications of its
own. In the end, though, Pip and Estella appear to
be heading into marriage.

13. Dickens incorporates sets of comparatively paired and
contrastingly foiled characters in the novel. Detail at
least one set of comparatively paired and one set of
contrastingly foiled characters.

Answers will vary. Comparisons of people in different social classes abound, but Dickens also contrasts
young Estella and Pip with older characters such as
Miss Havisham, Magwitch, and Joe.

14. "For a little piece I have been writing … such a very
fine, new, and grotesque idea has opened upon me."
"I have made the opening, I hope, in its general effect

exceedingly droll." (Charles Dickens speaks of *Great Expectations* in two letters to John Forster (531, 533). Dickens claimed this his novel was "grotesque," and employed that adjective proudly. Do you think there is anything grotesque about the novel? Explain.

> In the sense of "comically distorted," exaggerated and even strangely dark, students will find many instances of the grotesque in the novel, notably just about everything connected to Miss Havisham and Satis House.

15. Often, we wish we could go to a new place with a new situation to become the person we believe we would most like to be—to find and achieve our destiny. What kind of commentary on that dream might Dickens have for the reader today? Defend your answer with examples from the novel.

> This novel reminds the reader how easy it is to fall prey to false ideas and assumptions about other stations of life, especially in our youth. The answer is not to avoid one's dreams but to get good counsel and learn to appreciate the good one has before undervaluing it in the fire sale that dream-chasing may encourage.

16. Dickens was criticized for lack of humor in *A Tale of Two Cities* (his novel published just before *Great Expectations*). Although *A Tale of Two Cities* includes, arguably, quite a bit of humor (the "resurrection" man

who digs up dead bodies, the mighty Miss Pross, the many Jacques, etc.), Dickens did intend to stock plenty of humor in *Great Expectations*. Describe at least two characters you found humorous (be sure to treat what happened in a specific scene rather than speaking generally).

> Answers will vary. Wemmick and Mr. Pumblechook are good examples.

17. How do the opening and closing actions of the novel echo one another? What has changed?

> Pip and another character engage one another in a way that changes both their lives. In the opening, we have Pip and Magwitch; at the end, Pip and Estella. In both, Pip is walking among the reminders of a sad past, initially of the death of his parents and most siblings and finally of the fall of Satis House and the death of Miss Havisham. In both cases, the scene is set in the afternoon to evening. The difference is that Pip (and now Estella) has grown up and grown wiser; he is no longer so easy to threaten or dupe. Pip is no longer terrified by the world, but has found a true companion with whom to face the challenges of life.

18. Does Pip imply that he and Estella will marry or not marry at the conclusion of the novel?

> The final words of the novel—"I saw no shadow of parting from her"—imply that they will marry.

19. Here is the first draft of the final paragraphs of the novel. Dickens's good friend, Edward Bulwer-Lytton, read it and told him to change the conclusion. Read it and compare it to the published conclusion that you have in your book:

> It was four years more, before I saw herself [Estella]. I had heard of her as leading a most unhappy life, and as being separated from her husband who had used her with great cruelty, and who had become quite renowned as a compound of pride, brutality, and meanness.
>
> I had heard of the death of her husband (from an accident consequent on ill-treating a horse), and of her being married again to a Shropshire doctor, who, against his interest, had once very manfully interposed, on an occasion when he was in professional attendance on Mr. Drummle, and had witnessed some outrageous treatment of her. I had heard that the Shropshire doctor was not rich, and that they lived on her own personal fortune.
>
> I was in England again—in London, and walking along Piccadilly with little Pip—when a servant came running after me to ask would I step back to a lady in a carriage who wished to speak to me. It was a little pony carriage, which the lady was

driving; and the lady and I looked sadly enough on one another.

"I am greatly changed, I know; but I thought you would like to shake hands with Estella, too, Pip. Lift up that pretty child and let me kiss it!" (She supposed the child, I think, to be my child.)

I was very glad afterwards to have had the interview; for, in her face and in her voice, and in her touch, she gave me the assurance, that suffering had been stronger than Miss Havisham's teaching, and had given her a heart to understand what my heart used to be.[7]

How does that first draft ending differ from the final draft ending?

Pip and Estella speak for a brief minute but do not reunite (she already has remarried). Estella has aged severely due to abuse. Pip seems to have found no romantic love in life.

20. What do you think Dickens's friend told him?

Edward Bulwer-Lytton thought the original ending too sad and suggested the happy conclusion that Dickens finally decided upon.

---

7. Based on the proof slip reproduced by Edgar Rosenberg in the Norton Critical Edition of *Great Expectations* (New York: W.W. Norton, 1999), 492.

21. Which ending do you think fits better with the plot, characterization, and significant themes in the novel?

> Answers will vary. Many literary critics from the outset have defended the original ending as the superior in terms of plot, characterization, and themes.

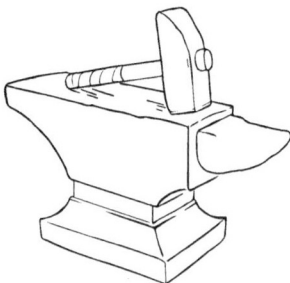

FURTHER DISCUSSION
AND REVIEW

Master what you have read by reviewing and integrating the different elements of this classic.

SETTING AND CHARACTERS
Be able to compare and contrast the personalities (including strengths, weaknesses, and mannerisms) of each character. Which characters change over the course of the novel? Which do not?

PLOT
Be able to describe the beginning, middle, and end of the book along with specific details that move the plot forward and make it compelling. Consider how Pip's plotline and other subplots (Compeyson and Magwitch seeking vengeance; Joe and Biddy growing in love; Miss Havisham's decay) all support the chief thread (Pip's transformation from naïve boy to thoughtful man).

CONFLICT

Although we find violence, subtle seduction, lies, and manipulation in the novel, a good case could be made that external conflict is eclipsed by internal conflict. Explain.

THEME STATEMENTS

"Money [is] the agent of isolation." ~ Walter Allen (writing of *Great Expectations*)

Consider various characters and their relationship to money. Notice the types of isolation that money breeds.

Forgiveness operates as the prime agent of change in the novel.

It is said that Fyodor Dostoevsky and Leo Tolstoy referred to Dickens as "that great Christian author." Indeed, one needn't look far to find a theme that resonates with our faith. The most glaring involves forgiveness. How is forgiveness the prime agent of change?

Although we are often encouraged to chase our dreams, whatever they may be, the truth is that those dreams may lead to nightmares when we greedily over-prize a new situation while thanklessly despising our own.

Pip secretly longs for higher social class, for the background that gives him the right to approach Estella on nearer terms, and, astonishingly, has all he could wish and more handed to him. Yet "money soon gained is soon squandered," and Pip has little to be proud of when he recollects how he employed his windfall. What might Dickens be representing about the way so many us long for richer lives?

Pip's life reflects a typical coming of age experience.

How are Pip's struggles common to us all, and what does his response to failure teach us?

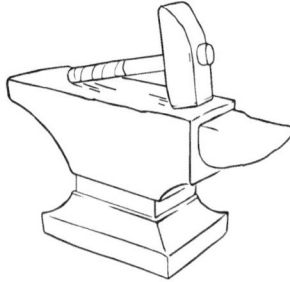

A NOTE FROM THE PUBLISHER:
TAKING THE CLASSICS QUIZ

Once you have finished the worldview guide, you can prepare for the end-of-book test. Each test will consist of a short-answer section on the book itself and the author, a short-answer section on plot and the narrative, and a long-answer essay section on worldview, conflict, and themes.

Each quiz, along with other helps, can be downloaded for free at www.canonpress.com/ClassicsQuizzes. If you have any questions about the quiz or its answers or the Worldview Guides in general, you can contact Canon Press at service@canonpress.com or 208.892.8074.

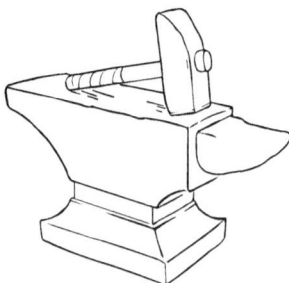

ABOUT THE AUTHOR

Marcus Schwager holds a Master's degree in Humanities from California State University, Dominguez Hills, writing his thesis on G. K. Chesterton. He and his wife, Meris, have five children and attend Trinity Covenant Church in Aptos, California. He writes for Canon Press, teaches upper-school Humanities at St. Abraham's Classical Christian Academy, and works for his family's construction and real estate company.

www.ingramcontent.com/pod-product-compliance
Lightning Source LLC
Chambersburg PA
CBHW070049040426
42331CB00034B/2864